nature's friends

Grasshoppers

by Ann Heinrichs

Content Adviser: Janann Jenner, Ph.D.

Science Adviser: Terrence E. Young Jr., M.Ed., M.L.S., Jefferson Parish (La.) Public Schools

Reading Adviser: Dr. Linda D. Labbo, Department of Reading Education, College of Education, The University of Georgia

COMPASS POINT BOOKS

MINNEAPOLIS, MINNESOTA

Compass Point Books
3722 West 50th Street, #115
Minneapolis, MN 55410

Visit Compass Point Books on the Internet at *www.compasspointbooks.com*
or e-mail your request to *custserv@compasspointbooks.com*

Photographs ©: Image Ideas, Inc., cover, 1; Robert McCaw, 4; Bill Glass/Root Resources, 6–7; Dwight R. Kuhn, 8–9, 14–15, 27; Leroy Simon/Visuals Unlimited, 10–11; Milton Rand/Tom Stack & Associates, 12–13; Kjell B. Sandved/Visuals Unlimited, 16; James P. Rowan, 18–19; Richard Demler, 20; Ken Lucas/Visuals Unlimited, 22–23; Gallo Images/Corbis, 24.

Editors: E. Russell Primm and Emily J. Dolbear
Photo Researchers: Svetlana Zhurkina and Jo Miller
Photo Selector: Linda S. Koutris
Designer: The Design Lab

Library of Congress Cataloging-in-Publication Data

Heinrichs, Ann.
    Grasshoppers / by Ann Heinrichs.
        p. cm. — (Nature's friends)
    Includes bibliographical references (p.   ).
    Summary: Introduces distinguishing characteristics, life cycles, and different types of grasshoppers.
    ISBN 0-7565-0166-0 (hardcover)
    1. Grasshoppers—Juvenile literature. [1. Grasshoppers.] I. Title. II. Series: Heinrichs, Ann. Nature's friends.
    QL508.A2 H43 2002
    595.7'26—dc21   2001004973

Printed in the United States of America.

Table of Contents

A Grasshopper's Day 5

A Grasshopper's Body 6

Kinds of Grasshoppers 9

Growing Up As a Grasshopper 10

Where Grasshoppers Live.................................13

How Grasshoppers Jump 14

Singing Grasshopper Songs 17

Dealing with Enemies 18

Grasshoppers As Pests 21

Locust Swarms.................................22

Grasshoppers for Lunch.................................25

Studying Grasshoppers.................................26

Glossary 28

Let's Look at Grasshoppers 29

Did You Know? 29

Junior Entomologists.................................30

Want to Know More? 31

Index 32

A Grasshopper's Day

Walk through a **meadow** on a sunny day. Listen, and you may hear a scratchy chirping sound. That's a grasshopper's "song." If you come too close, the grasshopper takes off with a giant jump.

An old tale tells about a lazy grasshopper. He sang all summer and did no work. When winter came, he had no food stored away. This would never really happen, though. Grasshoppers are busy eating all day.

◀ *A grasshopper rests on a plant.*

A Grasshopper's Body

The grasshopper's body is hard on the outside. The hard part is the **exoskeleton.** It protects the grasshopper's body.

A grasshopper has three main body parts—head, **thorax,** and abdomen. It has five eyes on its head. Three eyes are very small. The other two are huge **compound eyes.** Grasshoppers can see to the front, to the side, and to the back all at once. They cannot see colors—only light and dark.

Two antennae, or feelers, grow out of the grasshopper's head. They are used for smelling. A grasshopper uses its strong jaws to nibble grass.

On the thorax, grasshoppers have six legs. Most grasshoppers have four wings on the thorax, too.

Its stomach and egg-laying parts are inside a grasshopper's abdomen.

The grasshopper's body has three main parts. ▶

Kinds of Grasshoppers

Grasshoppers belong to **families.** One family is made up of short-horned grasshoppers. They have no horns—just short feelers.

Most of the grasshoppers we see jumping through the fields are short-horned. Locusts are short-horned grasshoppers, too. They are **migratory** insects. That means they move from one area to another.

Another family is made up of long-horned grass-hoppers. Their feelers can grow much longer than their bodies. Katydids are long-horned grasshoppers. Their name comes from the sound they make.

◀ *A short-horned grasshopper*

Growing Up a Grasshopper

A female grasshopper lays eggs in the ground or in rotten wood. She may lay more than 100 eggs at one time. Tiny babies called **nymphs** hatch out of the eggs. They look like grown-up grasshoppers. They are just smaller and have no wings.

As nymphs grow, they get too big for their shells. They molt, or shed that shell, and a new shell grows in its place. A nymph molts about four or five times. Finally it becomes an adult grasshopper with wings.

Grasshopper nymphs on a leaf ▶

Where Grasshoppers Live

Grasshoppers live almost everywhere in the world. Wherever grass grows, grasshoppers will find it!

Most grasshoppers live in fields and meadows. They eat grass and other leafy plants. For some grasshoppers, home is a tree. Katydids usually live in trees.

◄ A fork-tailed bush katydid

How Grasshoppers Jump

How tall are you? Let's say you are about 50 inches (127 centimeters) tall. Now let's pretend you are a grasshopper. If you were a grasshopper, and you were that tall, you could jump 1,000 inches (2,540 centimeters). That's more than 83 feet (25 meters). It's almost as long as a basketball court!

Grasshoppers use their powerful back legs for jumping. They can jump about twenty times their length. A 3-inch (7.6-centimeter) grasshopper can jump about 60 inches (152 centimeters), or 5 feet (1.5 meters).

A grasshopper jumping ▶

Singing Grasshopper Songs

Grasshoppers do not really sing. They make a chirping sound. Grasshoppers may chirp in one of two ways. Some rub their legs against their wings. Others rub two wings together.

Male grasshoppers usually chirp to attract a female mate. Sometimes they chirp to warn other males to stay away.

How do grasshoppers hear chirps? Some hear through holes on the sides of their body. Others hear through a hole on their legs!

◀ *A grasshopper's leg with a hole for hearing*

Dealing with Enemies

Frogs, birds, and lizards like to eat grasshoppers. Luckily, a grasshopper's color helps it hide from danger. Its color blends in with its surroundings.

Grasshoppers that live among leaves or in trees are green. Grasshoppers that live on the ground are brownish. Some grasshoppers live around sandy beaches. They are yellowish brown.

Grasshoppers can hop or fly away from their enemies. To scare an enemy away, a grasshopper may spit out a thick, brown liquid. Grasshoppers can bite their enemies, too.

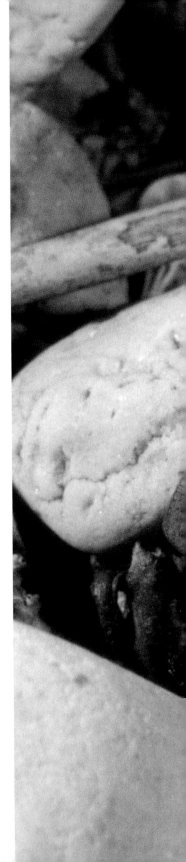

A Carolina locust blends in with its surroundings. ▶

Grasshopper Pests

Sometimes grasshoppers are pests! They may destroy a pretty flower garden. Or they may eat all the grass in a field where cows graze. They may wipe out a farmer's corn, hay, and other crops.

Grasshoppers become pests when there has not been much rain. Rain drowns many young insects. Without rain, too many young grasshoppers grow up. Some farmers use poison to kill them. Others bring in insects that eat grasshoppers.

◄ *Grasshoppers sometimes eat and destroy plants.*

Locust Swarms

Locusts are grasshoppers that travel in groups. When locusts cannot find enough food, they gather into crowds called swarms. Billions of locusts may join in a swarm. Across the land they go, eating just about every plant in sight.

Locust swarms can be scary! They darken the sky like a black cloud. Swarming locusts make a humming sound, too. In the past, locusts ruined farms all across the western United States.

A group of desert locusts ▶

Grasshoppers for Lunch

In some parts of the world, people eat grasshoppers. They remove the wings and legs before cooking them. They say grasshoppers make a tasty meal!

Grasshopper season is a happy time in some African villages. People come out at night and make fires. Thousands of grasshoppers are drawn to the firelight. Then the people scoop up the insects. They go home with big sacks full of grasshoppers. In the morning, they sell the grasshoppers in the market.

◀ *African children hold strings of lightly roasted grasshoppers that they hope to sell.*

Studying Grasshoppers

Scientists study grasshoppers. They want to learn how grasshoppers live, grow, and jump. You can learn a lot about grasshoppers, too.

You might keep a grasshopper for a pet. You should feed it grass, lettuce, and wheat **bran.** Keep a dish of water in its cage, too. But outdoors is the best place to watch grasshoppers. There you can see them jump. Try to see how far they can go!

Grasshopper eating grass ▶

Glossary

bran—the outer covering of a grain, such as wheat, that is sifted out when flour is made

compound eyes—eyes that are made up of many tiny eyes

exoskeleton—the hard covering on the outside of an animal's body that gives support and protection

families—groups of living things that have common characteristics

graze—to eat grass in a field

meadow—grassland that is usually moist, low-lying, and flat

migratory—having a lifestyle that includes moving from one region to another

nymphs—immature insects that differ from adult insects mainly in their size

thorax—the middle part of an insect's body

Let's Look at Grasshoppers

Long-Horned Grasshoppers
Class: Insecta
Order: Orthoptera
Family: Tettigoniidae

Short-Horned Grasshoppers
Class: Insecta
Order: Orthoptera
Family: Acrididae

Range: Grasshoppers are found throughout the world except for the coldest areas near the North Pole and the South Pole. The biggest variety of species is found in the tropics.

Life span: Grasshoppers live about one year.

Life stages: Most kinds of grasshoppers lay their eggs in soil. Grasshoppers have three life stages—egg, nymph, and adult.

Food: Grasshoppers are plant-eaters.

Did You Know?

Sometimes grasshopper nymphs form large groups and move together. During the 1800s in the United States, a migrating group was reported to be 23 miles (37 kilometers) wide and 70 miles (113 kilometers) long.

A large swarm of grasshoppers can be very destructive, eating all of a farmer's crops.

Female grasshoppers are usually larger than males.

Large swarms of grasshoppers have been known to destroy just about everything in their path—including clothes hanging on clotheslines and curtains hanging in windows.

Index

abdomen, 6

antennae, 6

body, 6

chirping, 5, 17

colors, 18

eggs, 10

exoskeleton, 6

eyes, 6

families, 9

food, 5, 6, 13, 25, 26

grasshopper season, 25

head, 6

jumping, 14, 26

katydids, 9, 13

legs, 6, 14

locusts, 9, 22

long-horned
  grasshoppers, 9

molting, 10

nymphs, 10

pests, 21

short-horned
  grasshoppers, 9

thorax, 6

About the Author: Ann Heinrichs grew up in Fort Smith, Arkansas. She began playing the piano at age three and thought she would grow up to be a pianist. Instead, she became a writer. Now she has written more than fifty books for children and young adults. Several of her books have won national awards. Ms. Heinrichs now lives in Chicago, Illinois. She enjoys martial arts and traveling to faraway countries.